TJG News

Regulating Digital Advertising Marketplaces

A research review

Tamaro Green

8/17/2022

Regulating Digital Advertising Marketplaces

Contents

Introduction

Digital advertising marketplaces have emerged from a number of contributing catalysts and incubating events. Innovation can bring products or services that become acceptable to the mainstream by virtue of their genius. These new products and services might rapidly replace existing products or services or create a new realm of commercial activity. Occurrences such as natural disasters, man-made conflicts, or health pandemics can create business opportunities that are chance situations for one company to dominate a market. Digital advertising marketplaces have developed as a commercial mode from innovation, globalization, and global events.

Market dominance may be very difficult to measure during events such as a pandemic. For example, customers may require a product or service during an emergency that does not give them the opportunity to choose from a variety of options. This may be one contributor to digital advertising dominance, especially if the dominance existed before the pandemic. Crises do not last forever and when they are over, the market for the specific product or service that was required may not be as large as it was during the crisis. Although, regulation could restrict the situation of dominant digital advertising marketplaces during a crisis, one approach is to let free markets restrict advertising dominance. Global events are learning opportunities and through planning and risk management the dependency on and reliability of digital advertising marketplaces may be governed through effective regulation.

Digital advertising markets may become extremely profitable during global events. Trends in industries can have large swings that enable companies that lead in a particular industry to extend their lead even further. This situation may be difficult to avoid as consumers may not have the time to evaluate all of their options when purchasing goods and services and would tend to flock to larger brands. Other businesses may not have the resources to develop competing goods and services during this time as the crisis is generally a resource constrained situation. The digital advertising markets appear to profit through global events as the market can also restrict competition. The market for products and services may determine the size and scale of the dominance influencing the need for regulation.

When regulation is required, digital advertising marketplaces may decide to thwart regulatory efforts. Regulating agencies may face challenges when competing with the lobbying efforts of large corporations. Lobbying efforts may encourage limited regulations for digital advertising marketplaces. Small businesses may have limited representation in designing legislation. This research will review the growth of multinational corporations through strategic alliances and international labour markets. Then it will discuss digital advertising as a major source of revenue from transitions in commerce. The research will discuss competition and antitrust regulation and the role of courts and agencies in regulating trade. Finally it will review recommendations for improving competition in digital advertising marketplaces.

Review of the growth of digital advertising marketplaces

Technology has provided solutions to problems and provided opportunities to expand commerce to digital advertising and marketing. The growth of digital advertising may be one of the benefits of technological innovation. Technology may have also presented limitations for society. For example, technology has provided opportunities for communication that may be a factor towards the instability of democracy as an institution (Eliassi-Rad et al., 2020). Eliassi-Rad et al. (2020) explore the features of a democracy in the representation of a complex system. One representation of democracy could be freedom of speech or equity of access.

Digital advertising marketplaces may provide a limitation on free market practices without regulation. Digital advertising marketplaces may follow trends in society where free speech is limited by market control. Eliassi-Rad et al. (2020) suggest that more research should pursue the potential backsliding of democracies. Wiesner et al. (2018) explain lower educational performance as an indicator for greater inequality. Cohen, Amarasingham, Shah, Xie, and Lo (2014) explain that educating consumers reduces liability in legal and ethical concerns of technology. Brown, Guin, and Morkoetter (2020) also include in their study education demographics for how people react during financial crises. Wiesner et al. (2018) describe how the lack of participation of researchers can contribute to financial crises.

The growth of digital advertising marketplaces has emerged from some of the improvements of technology in designing algorithms. Abebe, Kleinberg, and Parkes (2016) provide a mathematical solution to improve the cake cutting algorithm to allow for fair divisions of unequal parts. Technology may be a vice of technology for promoting inequalities or a tool for social change. Wiesner et al. (2018) describe a trend towards instability of democracies that is due to factors such as social inequality, financial crises, and disconnected information flows. Abebe et al. (2020) explains processes for which technology can be a vehicle for social change. Bender, Gebru, and McMillan-Major (2021) alert us to some of the dangers of technology without oversight.

Emerging digital advertising market places may profit from the prediction and modeling of data models of consumer data (Clarke, 2019; Zuboff, 2015). Clarke (2019) explores a transformation from relationships between customers and marketing corporations to data-reliant digital representations of customers. Zuboff (2015) examines how consumer data is monetized in marketing models based on prediction and modification of behaviour. Jacobides and Lianos (2021) describe the challenges for regulators in defining policies of emerging technology ecosystems.

The digital advertising marketplace may also be complex for regulation. The intricacies of technology ecosystems may present challenges for anti-trust regulators (Teece, 2020). Teece (2020) recommends reviewing organization economics to research anti-trust regulation and technology. Gao and Zhang (2021) explain goals of antitrust regulation should create healthy competition for market instead of focusing on punishment. Federico, Morton, and Shapiro (2019) provide examples in an exploration of the competition regulations on innovation.

Digital advertising marketplaces have strived from the resource of international and technological labour markets. Applications of artificial intelligence and machine learning may provide disruptors for labour markets (Alkomah & Ma, 2022; Rodríguez-Modroño, 2022).

Alkomah and Ma (2022) assess challenges in implementing artificial technology in practical review of online content. Kim (2022) proposes research models to improve multi-criteria decision making. Rodríguez-Modroño (2022) review advantages and disadvantages on the growth of teleworking in labour markets.

Assessment of Digital Advertising Marketplaces

One of the dangers of digital advertising marketplaces is the opportunity for companies that control technology to become business monopolies (Hovenkamp, 2020). Hovenkamp (2020) describes how the originality of digital platforms makes them difficult to regulate under antitrust laws. Monopolies may have a detrimental effect on economies by presenting a risk to innovation and entrepreneurship (Sokol, 2019). Wiesner et al. (2018) describe how economic stability can be representative of a democracy. Leitão and Ferreira (2021) explain that improving employment is only an initial stage of improving an economy.

The common thread of the development of digital advertising marketplaces is woven from the convenience for which technology provides. A digital advertising marketplace is a manifestation that transcends more than economic sectors of society. A digital advertising marketplace is able to control competition by having the power to determine which products or services to highlight. Digital advertising marketplaces have been able to control their platforms without oversight. In the history of American business the form and approach to competition regulation crosses the spectrum. The dangers of dominant digital advertising marketplace to a capitalist commercial system include damage to consumers and other businesses. The digital advertising marketplace through globalization and labour markets may dominate resources, labour, or manufactured goods, to encourage the sale of their products. However, a legal monopoly is a monopoly as defined by the antitrust code of United States law and monopolies are violations of federal law in the United States.

There may be psychological and physiological elements which have encouraged the development of dominant digital advertising marketplaces. Vaknin (2020) classifies narcissists and psychopaths to dissociate memories through a fictitious construct. Vaknin (2020) offers an explanation of the narcissist to have become a victimizer due to events from childhood that paralysed the ability of the ego. The psychological and physiological elements may also be areas to pursue for understanding the emergence of digital advertising marketplace dominance.

Mohammadpour-Yazdi and Jandl (2019) explores an ego for a group of people or nation through a shared system of idealized ideas. When a region fights for independence from a government, the parent government may be considered a colonizer. Struggles for independence in regions continue around the world. Ribeiro and Bussotti (2014) align collective anxiety around the independence movement on the continent to a climate for social and political instability in Africa.

Digital advertising marketplace dominance forms through control of resources. Capital, trademarks, and patents are areas where control of resource enables dominance. Lobbying influences regulators and courts on laws and policies regulating monopolies. The victimizing egotist can harm and may not self-restrict that ability (Vaknin, 2020). The id is a Freud's representation of primal passions. Self-regulation of a monopoly may prove similar to self-regulation of the id.

In the area of psychoanalysis, research continues in Freud's mode of cognition. However, further research may be required to comprehend the role of psychoanalysis in behaviours around information technology. Studies in neurobiology, computational biology, and neurology, may benefit from a social-psychological analysis of Internet behaviour. Human computer interaction may expand to human psychology computer interaction or computational neurobiology to psychological computational neurobiology. Carhart-Harris and Friston (2010) explore Freud's modes of cognition in neurobiology. Psychoanalysis of the Internet may include views on diversity and inclusion. Giordano (2020) applies Freud's modes of cognition to a literary analysis of female characters in two novels. Boag (2014) suggests personality structures are constructed from multiple instinctual drives and multiple egos.

Digital advertising marketplaces required a collaboration of a workforce that spanned the globe. However, the only profiteers from the effort were a small subset of the sample that skew the rewards and mask the creativity. Wiesner (2014) explains Freud's id to operate on a primordial pleasure principle geared to remove tension. Wiesner (2014) describes Freud's superego as the realm of moral judgements.

James (2016) compares the views of Sigmund Freud, and his contemporary Carl Jung, on the psychoanalysis of dreams. Freud's ego of the thinking active self in the collective systemic ambiguity of the Cartesian ego voids Jung's individualism. Watson (2014) reviews the concept of self and subject in philosophical history and Freud's modes of cognition. Possibly, the elimination of the concept of self in psychoanalysis may enable collective behaviour through fictitious constructs (Vaknin, 2020). The psychological elements of digital advertising marketplaces may provide benefit to understanding the limitations of exacting regulation and control.

Digital advertising marketplaces are also linked to the political applications of information communication technologies. The limitation of international organizations in addressing recent global crises presents opportunities to review their role in solving crisis situations. Cafaro (2017) discusses exogenous and endogenous contributions to views in supranational democracy. The exogenous contributions have been less challenging for international organizations in their ability to easily proclaim a common goal such as response to a natural disaster or military conflict. Endogenous debates may present struggles to the national characteristics of international organizations and are reinforced with social activism, petitions, and demonstrations (Cafaro, 2017). Cafaro (2017) provides the assurance that global democracy will not replace national democracy. An open mind to the ideal of global citizenship may enable the reality of a supranational international democratic organization.

Digital advertising marketplaces may also be influence by organizational culture. Corporate perception may have challenges in a global technological environment during the health pandemic (Lafuente, Marco, Monfort, & Ordóñez, 2022). Lafuente et al. (2022) measure and compare perceived corruption across countries. Pollák and Markovič (2022) suggest achieving transparency and information availability for corporate reputation management.

Cass (2013) explains how the complexity and uniqueness of technology companies and their business models make it difficult for legislators to develop antitrust regulations. Technology companies that have developed unique products may easily form dominance in that area. Technology also has a growing influence on consumer activity. As the information and communication sector grows, the increase reliance on the Internet for commerce makes it more and more difficult for consumers to conduct everyday activities without interaction with digital advertising marketplaces.

As convenience is introduced in an activity, the traditional method for that activity may become less available. Although, it is still possible to pay bills at an office, the availability is reduced by the ability to pay bills online. Online grocers have made hampered the business of traditional grocers. Ride sharing companies have reduced the availability of taxi services. Technology companies have even replaced other technology companies with more convenient services. Airline registration and travel sites face competition from companies that make searching airfares and booking hotels easier.

As digital advertising marketplaces becomes routine in everyday activities, marketplaces may assist consumers by developing practices of awareness of the impact that they are having on consumer experience and the limits that they are making on consumer choices. These marketplaces may also be supported by the generations that have already become accustomed to their participation in everyday activities. Digital advertising marketplaces may also respect fair competition practices by avoiding collusion.

One example of collusion is when companies work together to fix prices (Lande & Marvel, 2000). Lande and Marvel (2000) explain collusion to be one of the critical offenses for antitrust regulators to forbid.

The disruption of traditional consumer experiences through technological innovation has also influenced the automobile market (Crane, 2016). Crane (2016) describes antitrust challenges in the disruption of direct distribution of electronic vehicles as opposed to the sale of combustion vehicles from manufacturers that deliver through automobile dealers. The ability of a car dealer to sell cars without relying on automobile dealers also creates a situation where consumers may not receive competitive prices.

Horizontal and vertical mergers in technology may facilitate market dominance. Horizontal mergers occur when the two merging firms compete with one another

(Hovenkamp, 2020). An example of horizontal mergers in technology can be the large scale acquisition of social media platforms. Vertical mergers occur often in technology where larger firms purchase upcoming startups (Sokol, 2019). Sokol (2019) argues that regulating vertical mergers in technology would stifle technical innovation by restricting the ability for entrepreneurs to develop exit plans for startups.

Findings of Digital Advertising Marketplaces Research

Hovenkamp (2020) describe some of the strategies that may be implemented to reduce dominance on technology platforms such as interoperability, pooling data sources. Strategies such as these do not rely heavily on regulation. They may also allow for smaller companies to have greater chances of competing in new technological markets.

Cafaro (2017) acknowledges the challenges for replication the success of one international or regional organization to another in a different cultural climate. Cafaro (2017) also notes the economic and policy challenges of representative supranational democracy. Cafaro (2017) provides examples of how the roots of supranational democracy are fertilized within the limited realms of global creative spaces.

The global creative space in the rudimentary form of technology and social media networks has the opportunity to one day serve as a prototype for the supranational citizen model. Today, the participation of these tools in the global democracy, once seen as the obvious next step, is obscured by the security, privacy, and ethical issues of recent years.

Digital advertising marketplaces create shifts in labour and economic resources. A shift from low skilled workers to high skilled workers may be enhanced through the globalization of information communication technology. Wolcott (2020) identified that a shift in demand from workers without skills to workers with skills has contributed to employment inequality. The shifts in labour may also contribute to dominance in digital advertising marketplaces.

Digital advertising marketplaces may have an impact on periods of economic downturn. Financial policy implemented to mitigate economic risks may lead to a slower economic growth (Neanidis, 2019). Neanidis (2019) examine how prudent financial policies and regulations affect economic growth. The financial policies that reduce credit risk may prevent a situation such as the 2007 financial crisis. Salleo, Grassi, and Kyriakopoulos (2020) explain that the 2007 financial crisis demonstrated the importance of the banking sector for economic stability. Griffin, Kruger, and Maturana (2020) provide an empirical analysis of the influences to the housing boom and collapse at the time of the 2007 financial crisis and concur with academics that suggest that excess credit supply and investor speculation may have played a role in the housing collapse.

New techniques for financial models may assist in discovering economic policies for digital advertising marketplaces. Gupta, Dengre, Kheruwala, and Shah (2020) explain applications of text-mining for making financial predictions. Chaouki, Hardiman, Schmidt, Sérié, and de Lataillade (2020) explain how deep learning can be implemented for financial portfolio management by developing trading policies.

Rotella (2012) describes a shift in power to employers in periods of high unemployment which may explain conditions of higher productivity and economic growth. An example of higher productivity while maintaining high unemployment levels may be the effects of automation on labour markets. An increase in automation created higher levels of productivity, yet also replaced existing occupations. Pham and Vu (2022) define digital servitization as an information technology enabled integration of products and services and assess the sustainability of organizational practice. Improving practices and conditions in international labour may support sustainable digital advertising marketplaces.

Encouraging labour unions may also enhance competition in digital advertising marketplaces. Unions are an increasingly popular topic of discussion for digital advertising marketplaces. Employees of larger marketplaces have been collaborating to form unions. Some sectors of the technology industry have also commenced to form unions such as ride-sharing and communication. The influence of these unions on the policies, practices, and regulation of digital advertising marketplaces may have an impact in existing labour markets. Labour unions may advocate for regulation that restricts the size of technology companies. Posner, Weyl, and Naidu (2019) discuss a postulation of theory that explains that feudalism persevered in common law elements which allowed for employers to develop monopolies. Posner et al. (2019) also explain how unions pressured governments to develop laws that protected workers. Unions in technology companies may be a formidable ally in developing efficient and effective regulations to protect technology workers.

The unions may be a product of what digital advertising marketplace labour workers describe as mistreatment. Claims of harassment and mistreatment of workers by digital advertising marketplace workers may be a driving factor to what has given rise to the demand for unions. A rise in employment related class and collective action lawsuits across all labour markets may have also prompted the desire to form unions. Maatman (2017) analyses decisions from class and collective action claims under Title VII of the Civil Rights Act of 1964, the Age Discrimination in Employment Act, the Fair Labor Standards Act, and other related workplace federal statutes and predict growth in class and collective action litigation.

Motivation for unions may also be impacted by the practices of digital advertising marketplaces. Digital advertising marketplaces have earned public scrutiny for a number of practices such as mishandling consumer data and consumer privacy. Research that has involved the role of technology has also become more pervasive which stresses the limit of protection of human subjects in scientific research. Pisani et al. (2016) challenge technology research such as device monitoring, even with consent, as a potential risk to the protection of human subjects.

The increasing complexity of labour markets may also peripherally push for unions. Internationalization of labour markets and the growth of labour markets may persistently raise concerns for the need to regulate the emerging form of labour markets. Kanat, Hong, and Raghu (2018) highlight the growth of online labour markets and compare their effectiveness in developed and under-developed countries.

Unions may be able to play the part of a liason between not only workers and technology companies but can actively participate in the development of adequate legislation to protect workers. The government may be able to partner with unions to effectively deliver worker protection services. Collins and Gerlach (2019) showcase the rise of partnerships between governments and non-profit organizations in the delivery of services.

Unions may protect workers and support digital advertising marketplaces in producing corporate social responsibility. Sonntag and Spiller (2018) study how moral concerns affect public perception of corporate social responsibility. Protection of workers may be an effective way for technology companies to demonstrate to the public their commitment to corporate social responsibility.

Dubbink and van Liedekerke (2020) recommend that the principles of Kant can be implemented as criteria for moral purity in business, self-discipline, sacrifice, and moral pride. As business exists in a democracy, businesses should participate in the efforts to protect democracy in resource constrained environments. Eliassi-Rad et al. (2020) suggest as a policy recommendation to improve democracy to mandate representation and objectivity. Mandating harmony and tolerance for cultural diversity can also contribute to a healthy democracy.

The recommendation should also consider climate change concerns in any implementation for resource constrained environments. Espinoza and Aronczyk (2021) explain how corporate control of climate change concerns has led to a limited effort by corporations to address environmental issues. Espinoza and Aronczyk (2021) describe the "informating" of environmental issues by large corporations that focus on profit-oriented data practices to mitigate climate change. The policy recommendations should have an effective protocol for addressing the possibility of contributing to climate change.

Digital advertising marketplaces may disrupt traditional commerce and influence global economies (Gopalan, Reddy, & Sasidharan, 2022; Teachout, 2018). Gopalan et al. (2022) discover companies who participate in digitalization often also encourage global value chains. Alshubiri, Jamil, and Elheddad (2019) evaluated the impact of the development of information communication technologies on finance and economy sectors. Teachout (2018) explains how corporations can employ legal strategies to influence public officials and exploit financial power globally.

Emerging research evaluates recommendations to improve development and application of information communication technologies (de Munk, Scoccia, &

Malavolta, 2022; Rehse & Tremöhlen, 2022). Rehse and Tremöhlen (2022) make recommendations to increase trust in technology for encouraging digital contact tracing during health epidemics. de Munk et al. (2022) assess measures for testing software applications which run on mobile devices. Soliman, Avgeriou, and Li (2021) propose techniques for identifying software design decisions which potentially become costly when modifications are necessary.

Corporate perception may have challenges in a global technological environment during the health pandemic (Lafuente et al., 2022). Lafuente et al. (2022) measure and compare perceived corruption across countries. Pollák and Markovič (2022) suggest achieving transparency and information availability for corporate reputation management.

Digital advertising marketplaces may be viewed as monopolizing commerce with technology. An array of views examines the effectiveness of regulations for monopolies (Teachout, 2018). Teachout (2018) suggests concentrated power is the vice and not free and open markets. Vaheesan (2018) reviews consumer welfare models for antitrust regulation. Shafi, Sarker, and Junrong (2019) discuss the potential for small creative firms to strive in global economies.

Global digitalization has presented challenges in keeping the public from potential harm (Czarnocki, 2021). Wright and Zhu (2018) present risks to monopolistic influences through foreign direct investments. Kerber and Schweitzer (2017) assess interoperability in international technology regulation. Czarnocki (2021) compare international regulation to address challenges brought on by global digitalization.

Emerging research assesses influences to corporate market power in consumer markets (Chen & Nie, 2014; Cowan, 2018). Decker (2016) discusses challenges for regulators when shifts in demand for innovative services occur. Chen and Nie (2014) confirm business innovation slows when one or two companies have a greater percentage of market power. Cowan (2018) proposes the idea of regulating profit margins in consumer markets. Kärnä, Karlsson, Engberg, and Svensson (2022) explore the effects of product substitutability on innovation and market power.

Emerging technologies may prevent regulatory and ethical challenges for digital advertising marketplaces (Huberman, Leshno, & Moallemi, 2019). Huberman et al. (2019) explain how monopolistic and competitive components affect regulation of cryptocurrencies based on blockchain technologies. Abowd and Schmutte (2019) describe techniques for measuring privacy as properties of statistical algorithms. Kanat et al. (2018) describe global online labor markets as a disruptive technological force for local information technology labor markets.

Emerging digital marketing strategies may tend towards prediction and modeling of data models of consumer data (Clarke, 2019; Zuboff, 2015). Clarke (2019) explores a transformation from relationships between customers and marketing corporations to data-reliant digital representations of customers. Zuboff (2015) examines how consumer data is monetized in marketing models based on prediction and modification of behaviour. Jacobides and Lianos (2021) describe the challenges for regulators in defining policies of emerging technology ecosystems.

Studying renewable energy management may lead to improved energy conservation in the transportation and construction industries improving logistics for digital advertising marketplaces (Baral et al., 2019; Van Der Stelt, AlSkaif, & van Sark, 2018). Baral et al. (2019) conducts an economic analysis of logistics for resources in developing renewable energy sources in the aviation industry. Sahoo, Bilek, Bergman, and Mani (2019) also analyze the logistical costs of developing viable solutions for reducing financial and environmental costs of fuels with a sensitivity analysis. Vossos, Gerber, Bennani, Brown, and Marnay (2018) analyze and model cost saving techniques in applications of building direct current distribution commercial buildings. Van Der Stelt et al. (2018) explore theories in energy storage management for household energy storage systems and conduct a sensitivity analysis to determine the viability of the proposed systems.

Analysis of innovations in energy management may possibly provide alternatives to current techniques for power, cooling, and heating (Askari, Ameri, & Calise, 2018; Khosravi, Koury, Machado, & Pabon, 2018; Rufuss,

Kumar, Suganthi, Iniyan, & Davies, 2018). Khosravi et al. (2018) include solar and wind power in their analysis of energy management systems. Abadeh et al. (2018) conduct analyses of implementing nanofluids for cooling and explore the economic and environmental costs. Rufuss et al. (2018) apply fuzzy analytical hierarchy processing, capable of handling numerical or linguistic values, for predicting desalination models. Askari et al. (2018) explain exergo-economics as a measure of systems with somewhat steady operating systems. Askari et al. (2018) conduct an exergo-economic analysis to measure water, electricity, heating, and cooling costs in desalination and thermal vapor compression systems.

Emerging research may support evaluations of economic growth and sustainability of digitial advertising marketplaces (Liargovas & Pilichos, 2022). Liargovas and Pilichos (2022) review the effectiveness of fiscal policies developed to improve the sustainability of national economies. Jeke and Wanjuu (2021) provide an analysis of unemployment and inflation rates to determine a relationship between investment in human capital and economic growth. Brouwer and de Haan (2022) assess public awareness of the role of central banks in economic regulation. de Albuquerque, Caiado, and Pereira (2020) assess whether an increase in life expectancy influences inflation levels.

Conclusions and Recommendations

Research on sustainability may support effective ways to improve digital advertising marketplaces from the effects of globalization and international labour markets. Gancia, Ponzetto, and Ventura (2022) review the historical growth of globalization and observe the effects on country size, trade, and participation in international unions. Khabbazan and Hokamp (2022) provide simulations of sustainability models to review effectiveness of climate policies.

Digital advertising marketplaces may also be impacted by the growth of social media platforms. Emerging research examines the benefits and risks of social media networks (Özkent, 2022; Sedgwick, Epstein, Dutta, & Ougrin, 2019). Özkent (2022) analyze the influence of social media on the dissemination of scientific research information. Sedgwick et al. (2019) suggest longitudinal studies to determine the mental health issues associated with social media consumption. Rosenquist, Morton, and Weinstein (2022) review introducing antitrust regulation to reduce the risk to consumers of excessive social media consumption.

Trending research provides innovative strategies for measuring effectiveness of social network platform information dissemination (Atiq, Abid, Anwar, & Ijaz, 2022). Atiq et al. (2022) examine reliability and trust in the behaviors of social media influencer markets. French and Bazarova (2017) evaluate anticipated responses and characteristics of behaviors on social network platforms. Weeks, Lane, Kim, Lee, and Kwak (2017) review exposure to political news on social network platforms.

Digital advertising marketplaces may require new strategies for securing data, protecting consumers from harm and encouraging competition (Dwivedi et al., 2022;

Egan, 2022; O'Lawrence, Saunders, Li, & Kelly, 2018). Egan (2022) propose the need for comparative research to support privacy regulation of digitalization. Dwivedi et al. (2022) discusses challenges in privacy, information security, and ethics in the emerging technologies of virtual reality. O'Lawrence et al. (2018) provide an overview of the antitrust regulation in place for the health care industry.

Lobbying and antitrust legislation may serve to encourage healthy competition in digital advertising marketplaces (Holman & Luneburg, 2012; Larsson, 2021; Willson, 2020). Larsson (2021) reviews competition practices on digital platforms and presents challenges to fair competition where the digital marketplace providers are advertising their own products on their platforms. Willson (2020) explains the municipal importance and constitutional right of lobbying to coordinate policies of lawmakers with goals in scientific research. Holman and

Luneburg (2012) detail transparency as instrumental to lobbying regulation.

Intricacies of technology ecosystems may present challenges for anti-trust regulators (Teece, 2020). Teece (2020) recommends reviewing organization economics to research anti-trust regulation and technology. Gao and Zhang (2021) explain goals of antitrust regulation should create healthy competition for market instead of focusing on punishment. Federico et al. (2019) provide examples in an exploration of the competition regulations on innovation.

Emerging research evaluates recommendations to improve development and application of digital advertising marketplaces (de Munk et al., 2022; Rehse & Tremöhlen, 2022). Rehse and Tremöhlen (2022) make recommendations to increase trust in technology for encouraging digital contact tracing during health epidemics. de Munk et al. (2022) assess measures for testing software applications which run on mobile devices. Soliman et al. (2021) propose techniques for identifying software design decisions which potentially become costly when modifications are necessary.

Organizational change may improve the ability for digital advertising marketplaces to adapt with effective models (Kuehnel & Au-Yong-Oliveira, 2022; McKenzie, 2022). Kuehnel and Au-Yong-Oliveira (2022) suggest agile models for organizational structure for companies to adapt to consumer, manufacturing, and environmental demands more easily. Lv, Liu, and Xu (2019) demonstrate technology and globalization lead to lower growth in inflation. McKenzie (2022) proposes methods for evaluating influence in the entertainment industry.

References:

Abadeh, A., Rejeb, O., Sardarabadi, M., Menezo, C., Passandideh-Fard, M., & Jemni, A. (2018). Economic and environmental analysis of using metal-oxides/water nanofluid in photovoltaic thermal systems (PVTs). *Energy, 159*, 1234-1243.

Abebe, R., Barocas, S., Kleinberg, J., Levy, K., Raghavan, M., & Robinson, D. G. (2020). *Roles for computing in social change.* Paper presented at the Proceedings of the 2020 Conference on Fairness, Accountability, and Transparency.

Abebe, R., Kleinberg, J., & Parkes, D. (2016). Fair division via social comparison. *arXiv preprint arXiv:1611.06589.*

Abowd, J. M., & Schmutte, I. M. (2019). An economic analysis of privacy protection and statistical accuracy as social choices. *American Economic Review, 109*(1), 171-202.

Alkomah, F., & Ma, X. (2022). A literature review of textual hate speech detection methods and datasets. *Information, 13*(6). doi:10.3390/info13060273

Alshubiri, F., Jamil, S. A., & Elheddad, M. (2019). The impact of ICT on financial development: Empirical evidence from the Gulf Cooperation Council countries. *International Journal of Engineering Business Management, 11*, 1847979019870670. doi:10.1177/1847979019870670

Askari, I. B., Ameri, M., & Calise, F. (2018). Energy, exergy and exergo-economic analysis of different water desalination technologies powered by Linear Fresnel solar field. *Desalination, 425*, 37-67.

Atiq, M., Abid, G., Anwar, A., & Ijaz, M. F. (2022). Influencer marketing on Instagram: A sequential mediation model of storytelling content and audience engagement via relatability and trust. *Information, 13*(7). doi:10.3390/info13070345

Baral, N. R., Kavvada, O., Mendez-Perez, D., Mukhopadhyay, A., Lee, T. S., Simmons, B. A., & Scown, C. D. (2019). Techno-economic analysis and life-cycle greenhouse gas mitigation cost of five routes to bio-jet fuel blendstocks. *Energy & Environmental Science, 12*(3), 807-824.

Bender, E., Gebru, T., & McMillan-Major, A. (2021). On the dangers of stochastic parrots: Can language models be too big. *Proceedings of FAccT.*

Boag, S. (2014). Ego, drives, and the dynamics of internal objects. *Frontiers in Psychology, 5*(666). doi:10.3389/fpsyg.2014.00666

Brouwer, N., & de Haan, J. (2022). The impact of providing information about the ECB's instruments on inflation expectations and trust in the ECB: Experimental evidence. *Journal of Macroeconomics, 73*, 103430. doi:https://doi.org/10.1016/j.jmacro.2022.103430

Brown, M., Guin, B., & Morkoetter, S. (2020). Deposit withdrawals from distressed banks: Client relationships matter. *Journal of Financial Stability, 46*, 100707. doi:https://doi.org/10.1016/j.jfs.2019.100707

Cafaro, S. (2017). Democracy in international organizations: Arguments in support of a supranational approach. *The International Journal of Interdisciplinary Global Studies*(12), 7-19.

Carhart-Harris, R. L., & Friston, K. J. (2010). The default-mode, ego-functions and free-energy: a neurobiological account of Freudian ideas. *Brain, 133*, 1265–1283.

Cass, R. A. (2013). Antitrust and high-tech: Regulatory risks for innovation and competition. *Engage, 14*(1), 25-32.

Chaouki, A., Hardiman, S., Schmidt, C., Sérié, E., & de Lataillade, J. (2020). Deep deterministic portfolio optimization. *The Journal of Finance and Data Science, 6*, 16-30. doi:https://doi.org/10.1016/j.jfds.2020.06.002

Chen, Y.-h., & Nie, P.-y. (2014). Duopoly innovation under product externalities. *Economic Research-Ekonomska Istraživanja, 27*(1), 232-243. doi:10.1080/1331677X.2014.952092

Clarke, R. (2019). Risks inherent in the digital surveillance economy: A research agenda. *Journal of Information Technology, 34*(1), 59-80. doi:10.1177/0268396218815559

Cohen, I. G., Amarasingham, R., Shah, A., Xie, B., & Lo, B. (2014). The legal and ethical concerns that arise from using complex predictive analytics in health care. *Health Affairs, 33*(7), 1139-1147. doi:10.1377/hlthaff.2014.0048

Collins, T., & Gerlach, J. D. (2019). Bridging the gaps: Local government and nonprofit collaborations. *Journal of Public and Nonprofit Affairs, 5*(2), 118-133.

Cowan, S. (2018). Regulating monopoly price discrimination. *Journal of Regulatory Economics, 54*(1), 1-13. doi:10.1007/s11149-018-9361-2

Crane, D. A. (2016). Tesla, dealer franchise laws, and the politics of crony capitalism. *University of Michigan Law School Scholarship Repository, 101*(2), 573-607.

Czarnocki, J. (2021). Saving EU digital constitutionalism through the proportionality principle and a transatlantic digital accord. *European View, 20*(2), 150-156. doi:10.1177/17816858211055522

de Albuquerque, P. C. A. M., Caiado, J., & Pereira, A. (2020). Population aging and inflation: Evidence from panel cointegration. *Journal of Applied*

Economics, 23(1), 469-484. doi:10.1080/15140326.2020.1795518

de Munk, O., Scoccia, G. L., & Malavolta, I. (2022). The state of the art in measurement-based experiments on the mobile web. *Information and Software Technology*, 106944. doi:https://doi.org/10.1016/j.infsof.2022.106944

Decker, C. (2016). Regulating networks in decline. *Journal of Regulatory Economics, 49*(3), 344-370. doi:10.1007/s11149-016-9300-z

Dubbink, W., & van Liedekerke, L. (2020). Rethinking the purity of moral motives in business: Kant against moral purism. *Journal of Business Ethics, 167*(3), 379-393. doi:10.1007/s10551-019-04167-y

Dwivedi, Y. K., Hughes, L., Baabdullah, A. M., Ribeiro-Navarrete, S., Giannakis, M., Al-Debei, M. M., . . . Wamba, S. F. (2022). Metaverse beyond the hype: Multidisciplinary perspectives on emerging challenges, opportunities, and agenda for research, practice and policy. *International Journal of Information Management, 66*, 102542. doi:https://doi.org/10.1016/j.ijinfomgt.2022.102542

Egan, M. (2022). Privacy boundaries in digital space: an exercise in responsibilisation. *Information & Communications Technology Law*, 1-18. doi:10.1080/13600834.2022.2097046

Eliassi-Rad, T., Farrell, H., Garcia, D., Lewandowsky, S., Palacios, P., Ross, D., . . . Wiesner, K. (2020). What science can do for democracy: A complexity science approach. *Humanities and Social Sciences Communications, 7*(1), 30. doi:10.1057/s41599-020-0518-0

Espinoza, M. I., & Aronczyk, M. (2021). Big data for climate action or climate action for big data? *Big Data & Society, 8*(1), 2053951720982032. doi:10.1177/2053951720982032

Federico, G., Morton, F. S., & Shapiro, C. (2019). Antitrust and innovation: Welcoming and protecting disruption. *Innovation Policy and the Economy, 20*, 125-190. doi:10.1086/705642

French, M., & Bazarova, N. N. (2017). Is anybody out there?: Understanding masspersonal communication through expectations for response across social media platforms. *Journal of Computer-Mediated Communication, 22*(6), 303-319. doi:https://doi.org/10.1111/jcc4.12197

Gancia, G., Ponzetto, G. A. M., & Ventura, J. (2022). Globalization and political structure. *Journal of the European Economic Association, 20*(3), 1276-1310. doi:10.1093/jeea/jvac019

Gao, R., & Zhang, F. (2021, 2021-08-04T19:29:46.000Z). *Research on anti-monopoly regulations of internet platforms in China and comments on the "Anti-Monopoly Guidelines on the Platform Economy Field".*

Giordano, G. (2020). The contribution of Freud's theories to the literary analysis of two Victorian novels: Wuthering Heights and Jane Eyre. *International Journal of English and Literature, 11*(2), 29-34.

Gopalan, S., Reddy, K., & Sasidharan, S. (2022). Does digitalization spur global value chain participation? Firm-level evidence from emerging markets. *Information Economics and Policy*, 100972. doi:https://doi.org/10.1016/j.infoecopol.2022.100972

Griffin, J. M., Kruger, S., & Maturana, G. (2020). What drove the 2003–2006 house price boom and subsequent collapse? Disentangling competing explanations. *Journal of Financial Economics*. doi:https://doi.org/10.1016/j.jfineco.2020.06.014

Gupta, A., Dengre, V., Kheruwala, H. A., & Shah, M. (2020). Comprehensive review of text-mining applications in finance. *Financial Innovation, 6*(1), 39. doi:10.1186/s40854-020-00205-1

Holman, C., & Luneburg, W. (2012). Lobbying and transparency: A comparative analysis of regulatory reform. *Interest Groups & Advocacy, 1*(1), 75-104. doi:10.1057/iga.2012.4

Hovenkamp, H. J. (2020). Antitrust and platform monopoly. *Faculty Scholarship at Penn Law*, 2192.

Huberman, G., Leshno, J., & Moallemi, C. C. (2019). An economic analysis of the Bitcoin payment system. *Columbia Business School Research Paper*(17-92).

Jacobides, M. G., & Lianos, I. (2021). Ecosystems and competition law in theory and practice. *Industrial and Corporate Change, 30*(5), 1199-1229. doi:10.1093/icc/dtab061

James, L. (2016). Carl Jung's Psychology of Dreams and His View on Freud. *Acta Psychopathologica, 2*(3).

Jeke, L., & Wanjuu, L. Z. (2021). The economic impact of unemployment and inflation on output growth in South Africa. *Journal of Economics and International Finance, 13*(3), 117-126.

Kanat, I., Hong, Y., & Raghu, T. (2018). Surviving in global online labor markets for IT services: a geo-economic analysis. *Information Systems Research, 29*(4), 893-909.

Kärnä, A., Karlsson, J., Engberg, E., & Svensson, P. (2022). Political failure: A missing piece in innovation policy analysis. *Economics of Innovation and New Technology*, 1-32. doi:10.1080/10438599.2022.2070843

Kerber, W., & Schweitzer, H. (2017). Interoperability in the digital economy. *JIPITEC, 8*(1), 39-58.

Khabbazan, M. M., & Hokamp, S. (2022). Decarbonizing the global economy: Investigating the role of carbon emission inertia using the integrated assessment model MIND. *Economies, 10*(8). doi:10.3390/economies10080186

Khosravi, A., Koury, R., Machado, L., & Pabon, J. (2018). Energy, exergy and economic analysis of a hybrid renewable energy with hydrogen storage system. *Energy, 148*, 1087-1102.

Kim, S. (2022). Critical success factors evaluation by multi-criteria decision-making: A strategic information system planning and strategy-as-practice perspective. *Information, 13*(6). doi:10.3390/info13060270

Kuehnel, K., & Au-Yong-Oliveira, M. (2022). The Development of an Information Technology Architecture for Automated, Agile and Versatile Companies with Ecological and Ethical Guidelines. *Informatics, 9*(2). doi:10.3390/informatics9020037

Lafuente, J. Á., Marco, A., Monfort, M., & Ordóñez, J. (2022). Does perceived corruption converge? International evidence. *Economics, 16*(1), 43-56. doi:doi:10.1515/econ-2022-0018

Lande, R. H., & Marvel, H. P. (2000). The three types of collusion: Fixing prices, rivals, and rules. *ScholarWorks University of Baltimore School of Law.*

Larsson, S. (2021). Putting trust into antitrust? Competition policy and data-driven platforms. *European Journal of Communication, 36*(4), 391-403. doi:10.1177/02673231211028358

Leitão, J., & Ferreira, J. (2021). Dynamic effects of material production and environmental sustainability on economic vitality indicators: A panel VAR approach. *Journal of Risk and Financial Management, 14*(2). doi:10.3390/jrfm14020074

Liargovas, P., & Pilichos, V. (2022). Is EU Fiscal Governance Effective? A Case Study for the Period

1999–2019. *Economies, 10*(8). doi:10.3390/economies10080187

Lv, L., Liu, Z., & Xu, Y. (2019). Technological progress, globalization and low-inflation: Evidence from the United States. *PLoS One, 14*(4), e0215366. doi:10.1371/journal.pone.0215366

Maatman, G. (2017). Annual workplace class action litigation report: An overview of 2016 in workplace class action litigation. *LABOR LAW JOURNAL*, 11-45.

McKenzie, J. (2022). The economics of movies (revisited): A survey of recent literature. *Journal of Economic Surveys, n/a*(n/a). doi:https://doi.org/10.1111/joes.12498

Mohammadpour-Yazdi, A.-R., & Jandl, M. (2019). Superego and will to dominate over ego: A synthetic approach to ideology through encapsulated skin-ego. *Language and Psychoanalysis, 8*(2), 61-79.

Neanidis, K. C. (2019). Volatile capital flows and economic growth: The role of banking supervision. *Journal of Financial Stability, 40*, 77-93. doi:https://doi.org/10.1016/j.jfs.2018.05.002

O'Lawrence, H., Saunders, L., Li, M., & Kelly, M. (2018). Health Policy Analysis: Antitrust Law and Regulation on Health Care Providers. *European Journal of Environment and Public Health, 2*(1).

Özkent, Y. (2022). Social media usage to share information in communication journals: An analysis of social media activity and article citations. *PLoS One, 17*(2), e0263725. doi:10.1371/journal.pone.0263725

Pham, H. Q., & Vu, P. K. (2022). Unravelling the potential of digital servitization in sustainability-oriented organizational performance -does digital leadership make it different? *Economies, 10*(8). doi:10.3390/economies10080185

Pisani, A. R., Wyman, P. A., Mohr, D. C., Perrino, T., Gallo, C., Villamar, J., . . . Brown, C. H. (2016). Human subjects protection and technology in prevention science: Selected opportunities and challenges. *Prev Sci, 17*(6), 765-778. doi:10.1007/s11121-016-0664-1

Pollák, F., & Markovič, P. (2022). Challenges for corporate reputation—online reputation management in times of global pandemic. *Journal of Risk and Financial Management, 15*(6). doi:10.3390/jrfm15060250

Posner, E. A., Weyl, G., & Naidu, S. (2019). Antitrust remedies for labor market power. *Harvard Law Review, 132*(2).

Rehse, D., & Tremöhlen, F. (2022). Fostering participation in digital contact tracing. *Information Economics and Policy, 58*, 100938. doi:https://doi.org/10.1016/j.infoecopol.2021.100938

Ribeiro, G. M., & Bussotti, L. (2014). Historical details on Freud and the moral order foundations of societies. *Advances in Historical Studies, 3*, 258-268.

Rodríguez-Modroño, P. (2022). Working conditions and work engagement by gender and digital work intensity. *Information, 13*(6). doi:10.3390/info13060277

Rosenquist, J. N., Morton, F. M. S., & Weinstein, S. N. (2022). Addictive Technology and Its Implications for Antitrust Enforcement. *NORTH CAROLINA LAW REVIEW, 100*, 431-486.

Rotella, E. J. (2012). Labor policy and the Great Recession: An economist's perspective. *Indiana Law Journal, 87*(1).

Rufuss, D. D. W., Kumar, V. R., Suganthi, L., Iniyan, S., & Davies, P. (2018). Techno-economic analysis of solar stills using integrated fuzzy analytical hierarchy process and data envelopment analysis. *Solar Energy, 159*, 820-833.

Sahoo, K., Bilek, E., Bergman, R., & Mani, S. (2019). Techno-economic analysis of producing solid biofuels and biochar from forest residues using portable systems. *Applied Energy, 235*, 578-590.

Salleo, C., Grassi, A., & Kyriakopoulos, C. (2020). A comprehensive approach for calculating banking sector risks. *International Journal of Financial Studies, 8*(4). doi:10.3390/ijfs8040069

Sedgwick, R., Epstein, S., Dutta, R., & Ougrin, D. (2019). Social media, internet use and suicide attempts in adolescents. *Current Opinion in Psychiatry, 32*(6).

Shafi, M., Sarker, M. N. I., & Junrong, L. (2019). Social network of small creative firms and its effects on innovation in developing countries. *SAGE Open, 9*(4), 2158244019898248. doi:10.1177/2158244019898248

Sokol, D. D. (2019). Vertical mergers and entrepreneurial exit. *Florida Law Review, 70*(6), 5.

Soliman, M., Avgeriou, P., & Li, Y. (2021). Architectural design decisions that incur technical debt — An industrial case study. *Information and Software Technology, 139*, 106669. doi:https://doi.org/10.1016/j.infsof.2021.106669

Sonntag, I. W., & Spiller, A. (2018). Measuring public concerns? Developing a moral concerns scale regarding non-product related process and production methods. *Sustainability, 10*(5). doi:10.3390/su10051375

Teachout, Z. (2018). The Problem of Monopolies & Corporate Public Corruption. *Daedalus, 147*(3), 111-126. doi:10.1162/daed_a_00514

Teece, D. J. (2020). Innovation, governance, and capabilities: implications for competition policy: A Tribute to Nobel Laureate Oliver Williamson by his

Colleague and Mentee David J. Teece. *Industrial and Corporate Change, 29*(5), 1075-1099. doi:10.1093/icc/dtaa043

Vaheesan, S. (2018). The twilight of the technocrats' monopoly on antitrust? *The Yale Law Journal, 127*, 980-995.

Vaknin, S. (2020). Dissociation and confabulation in narcissistic disorders. *Journal of Addiction & Addictive Disorders*.

Van Der Stelt, S., AlSkaif, T., & van Sark, W. (2018). Techno-economic analysis of household and community energy storage for residential prosumers with smart appliances. *Applied Energy, 209*, 266-276.

Vossos, V., Gerber, D., Bennani, Y., Brown, R., & Marnay, C. (2018). Techno-economic analysis of DC power distribution in commercial buildings. *Applied Energy, 230*, 663-678.

Watson, A. (2014). Who am i? The self/subject according to psychoanalytic theory. *SAGE Open, 4*(3), 2158244014545971. doi:10.1177/2158244014545971

Weeks, B. E., Lane, D. S., Kim, D. H., Lee, S. S., & Kwak, N. (2017). Incidental exposure, selective exposure, and political information sharing: Integrating online exposure patterns and expression on social media. *Journal of Computer-Mediated Communication, 22*(6), 363-379. doi:https://doi.org/10.1111/jcc4.12199

Wiesner, J. L. (2014). Mental freedom: Who has control- the rider or the horse? *International Journal of Dharma Studies, 2*(7).

Wiesner, K., Birdi, A., Eliassi-Rad, T., Farrell, H., Garcia, D., Lewandowsky, S., . . . Thébault, K. (2018). Stability of democracies: A complex systems perspective. *European Journal of Physics, 40*(1), 014002. doi:10.1088/1361-6404/aaeb4d

Willson, P. D. (2020). The Importance of Lobbying to Advance Health and Science Policy. *Academic Medicine, 95*(1).

Wolcott, E. L. (2020). Employment inequality: Why do the low-skilled work less now? *Journal of Monetary Economics*. doi:https://doi.org/10.1016/j.jmoneco.2020.09.004

Wright, J., & Zhu, B. (2018). Monopoly rents and foreign direct investment in fixed assets. *International Studies Quarterly, 62*(2), 341-356. doi:10.1093/isq/sqy010

Zuboff, S. (2015). Big other: Surveillance capitalism and the prospects of an information civilization. *Journal of Information Technology, 30*(1), 75-89. doi:10.1057/jit.2015.5

www.ingramcontent.com/pod-product-compliance
Lightning Source LLC
LaVergne TN
LVHW050347160826
845677LV00014B/3842

* 9 7 9 8 8 4 7 1 8 7 3 4 3 *